THE WORLD FOLKTALE LIBRARY

Tales from the United States

Tales from the United States

By John Greenway

Illustrated by Susan Perl

Consultant
Moritz A. Jagendorf
Author and Folklorist

SILVER BURDETT COMPANY
Morristown, New Jersey
Glenview, Ill. • Palo Alto • Dallas • Atlanta

Library of Congress Catalog Card Number: 78-54626   ISBN 0-382-03351-5

INTRODUCTION

Folktales are not usually about real people or actual events, but in a way they are almost always true. They tell us something real about the people who make them up and pass them along. Folktales express the values of a society, and reveal that society's ideas about living and surviving.

These American tales express something true about your country and its people. To your ancestors, this new land seemed like an enormous place. Everything about it was gigantic. It was unfamiliar and lonely, and that loneliness was huge. There were many hardships to overcome and those hardships were giant-size. Even the animals and the people seemed twice as large (and as tall) as life.

In these tales you can discover the truth about how American pioneers brought a giant-size spirit and a larger-than-life courage to this land. They liked to laugh and joke about how bad things were—it made life easier. And they liked to boast and brag about the big spirit and the big people who overcame those hardships.

The stories about John Henry and Davy Crockett, for example, are based on legends about people who actually lived. Colonel Davy Crockett really did have a gun named Betsy, and in 1827 he did go to Washington as a congressman. He may not have wrestled a grizzly bear, but he did have the spirit to do it. And that's true.

THE EDITOR

To Joan and Jamie

CONTENTS

The Horse That Sat on Cabbages

On the day the horse fair opened, I saw Simon Hooter coming down the road soaking wet and grumbling to himself. I knew he had been slickered again. Now Simon Hooter was a smart enough fellow in most things. But every time he traded for a horse, he got slickered. He never learned. You might say that there was something about horses that froze his brains. Every time the horse fair came around, it happened again. The horse traders that slickered him were honest enough. I mean "honest" if you knew that what they said usually had more than one meaning. Simon Hooter always took the meaning he wanted to take. And he always got slickered.

Well, last time the horse fair was down this way, Simon walked around all the horses that were up for sale. He saw a little bay Morgan going for only twenty-five dollars. "What's wrong with it," he asked, "that it's sellin' for only twenty-five dollars?"

"He don't look so good," replied the trader. "He just don't look so good."

"Looks good enough to me," said Simon, and he handed over the twenty-five dollars and threw a saddle on the Morgan. He mounted, and before the horse had gone fifty yards, it walked into a tree and threw Simon on the ground. Simon cussed a bit, but he got back on. Then the horse walked into a fence. About that time Simon saw what was wrong with the horse, and he stomped back to the trader.

"That there horse is blind!" Simon yelled, shaking his fist in the trader's face.

"I told you he didn't *look* so good," said the trader. He had told the truth, sure enough, even though it was a little narrow.

Why, Simon even got slickered when he paid to *look* at horses. I remember the time the carnival came through here and Simon paid fifty cents to see the horse with its head where its tail ought to be. When Simon got into the tent, they just had a horse standing backward in the stall. You see what I mean? He got slickered every time. That's why I knew what had happened when I saw him coming down the road, wet as a hen with the hose turned on it, and just as mad.

"What happened to you, Simon?" I asked him.

"Tar-*nation*," he bawled, kicking a rock off the road. "I got slickered again at the horse fair, tarnate the tarnated luck!"

"How'd that happen, Simon?" I asked.

"Well," he said, sitting down on a rock to empty water out of his boots. "I seed this here Tennessee walkin' horse. I always wanted one of them walkin' horses, ever since I heard of 'em. And this one was cheap — cheap as a good mule.

"So I looked him over. I looked at his teeth, and they was all there, and they was in good shape. I looked at his eyes, and they was sharp. Ain't nobody goin' to sell me a blind horse agin! I took off the saddle, and there wasn't no saddle sores. Then I rode him 'round a bit, and he was perfect. So I said to the trader, 'All right, what's the matter with him?'

"The trader frowned, just like he had to say somethin' he didn't want to. 'I'll tell you,' he said after a while, 'this here horse has got a bad habit. He sits on cabbages. You might be ridin' along the road just as proud as old Squire

Mayfield, and on a sudden the horse will sit down and pitch you off into the ditch. Then you feel under the horse, and derned if you won't find he's set down on a cabbage.'

" 'Shucks,' I said to him, 'that won't bother me none. They ain't so many cabbages around here. Might be years 'fore he sets himself on a cabbage. If that's all that's wrong with him, mister, I'll just give you these here fifty dollar bills and I've got me a gen-u-wine Ten-no-see walkin' horse.'

"So we shook hands on the deal and I climbed up the stirrup and rode off. Went fine as you like, he did. Nary a thing wrong. Then we come to Four-Mile Creek, where you got to ford across ever since the bridge washed out last year. Only about two foot deep, so I just nudged the horse with my heels and in he went. And then, dod drot his skin, that horse sat down right in the middle of that creek. Pitched me into the water head over heels and hip over thigh.

"Well, I tell you, I cussed out that horse good and proper. Then I reached around under him in the mud feelin' for that pesky cabbage. But derned if there was any cabbage there. No cabbage at all. I got squilched with mud feelin' around for it. Well, I give that horse such a kick that he humped hisself up and he run off up toward Tennessee, where he come from. Then I tramped back to the horse fair and collared that there trader.

" 'Consarn your hide,' I says to him. 'That there horse you sold me sat down right in the middle of the creek. I'm filled full of water like a frog in floodtime. And there wasn't no cabbage in that creek for him to sit on. What you got to say about that?'

"The horse trader looked kinda sheepish, like. 'Mr. Hooter,' he says, 'Why, the horse is as good as gold. He just has that there bad habit, like I told you. He sits on cabbages. Onliest thing, I forgot to tell you he sits on fish, too!' "

Whar's Joe?

Everybody has heard of boys who have grown too big for their clothes. But who has heard of clothes that have grown too big for their boys? You don't see such clothes every day, and it's a good thing, too, considering what happened to poor Joe Meriwether. Joe's clothes grew too big for him, and that's why people down in Kentucky still ask ,"Whar's Joe?"

Joe and his big brother Bill lived on a farm in southern Kentucky, not very long after Daniel Boone had led the settlers into that beautiful state. That was when the woods were still full of Indians and bears and other exciting things. Young men had to grow up fast in those days, and Joe Meriwether tried hard to become a man as quickly as he could. He wore clothes that only a grown man should wear. And that's what got Joe into all this trouble.

Joe's brother, Bill Meriwether, was pretty nearly a man. In fact, Bill was so nearly a man that their father let him take the horse and wagon whenever there was stock or produce to sell in town. Usually Bill would drive the wagon up to Booneville, where old Widow Harris owned the general store. Young Joe went along, although he was too small to be a great help to Bill. But he was a good and smiling boy, and the Widow Harris always had a stick of licorice or a piece of rock candy for him when she heard the Meriwether horse clopping down the dusty road. The Meriwether boys would come to town every month or so, and Mrs. Harris would wave and holler from her rocking chair on the porch of her store.

"Halloo, Bill Meriwether!" she would call. "Whar's Joe?" And Joe would pop up from the bed of the wagon and wave back to her.

But one day when she called out "Halloo, Bill Meriwether! Whar's Joe?" no Joe popped up to wave at her.

"Whar's Joe, Bill?" she asked again, when Bill had tied the horse to the hitching bar on the porch.

Bill hung down his head. Two big tears rolled slowly down his cheeks, cutting a path through the dust. "He's gone, ma'am," Bill said, and his lip quivered as he tried not to cry.

"My sakes! Is he dead, poor boy? Did a b'ar or an Injun get him, poor darling?"

"I don't rightly know, Mrs. Harris, ma'am," answered Bill, wiping the tears and dust across his face with the back of his sleeve.

"Then whar is he? He hasn't gone and went to Californy, has he, poor darling?"

"He might could have gone to Californy, ma'am," said Bill. "Joe was heading that way the last I seen him."

"Merciful powers!" shuddered the Widow Harris. "Don't that boy know thar's two thousand miles full of Injuns and b'ars between here and Californy? How does that boy expect to walk through that kind of country?"

"Well, ma'am," sniffled Bill, "Brother Joe wasn't walkin, I reckon."

"Not walking? What did he ride, then — your pappy's mule? Why, we all know that thar mule ain't much better'n walking."

"No, ma'am, Mrs. Harris, ma'am. He wasn't riding, neither," said Bill, and two more tears plopped into the dust in front of the store.

"Bill Meriwether, don't you go funning a poor old widow woman with all that silly talk. If he wasn't riding and he wasn't walking, how was he going?"

Bill looked a little puzzled. He wasn't sure how to answer her. "Well, ma'am," Bill began, "he was rolling, like. Well, maybe not rolling, exactly. He was whirling, like. Yes, ma'am, that's it. He was whirling and somersaulting like a pinwheel."

"Gracious! Bless your poor head, Bill Meriwether. What on earth are you talking about? Have you been chawin' on your pappy's tobacker again?"

"No, ma'am, that's the way Brother Joe went. Like a pinwheel, with his arms and legs stuck right out, and whirling down the road."

"Lawk!" exclaimed the Widow Harris. She took Bill Meriwether by the arm, led him up on the porch, and sat him down in the rocking chair. "Now you tell a body whar's Joe, and no more tomfoolery."

"Tain't foolery, ma'am," said Bill, and he put his head in his hands. It was hard to be so nearly a man, but still a boy. He wiped his sleeve across his face again. "Mrs. Harris, ma'am," he said finally, "you remember how Brother Joe liked to dress himself up in them long britches and red neckershers that made him look like a grown man? You remember that, don't you?"

"Sakes, boy, I remember Joe like I remember you. I recollect all about the way he dressed. Sure, he dressed hisself like he were a grown man, but that was all right. But I don't see what that has to do with whar Joe is."

"Well, ma'am," sighed Bill, "it was the britches that did it to him. He got him a pair of new buckskin britches, the kind with the straps that go under your feet. Well, we was working down in the swamp, digging out a new ditch. The water was up near to our waist most the time, and Joe got them britches pretty wet." Bill stopped and shook his head for a moment as he remembered what happened.

"Yes, ma'am, he got them britches pretty wet. So he stood up close to the campfire while I was cooking a possum for dinner, and pretty soon that buckskin started to steam and dry and shrink up. You know how green buckskin shrinks when it gets wet and hot.

"Pretty soon it seemed to me as if Joe was growing. I knowed he was a healthy boy, but he looked to be growing even while I was watching him. I stood up, and derned if he wasn't looking me straight in the eye. 'What are you looking me straight in the eye for, Brother Joe?' I asked him. 'You know you're only four-feet-nothing in your bare toe-bones, and you can't look me in the eye unless you stand on something.' But while I was talking to him, he grew up a little more, like, and pretty soon he was looking me in the hat. I looked down to see what he was standing on, to see what was lifting him up. And gosh-a-mighty, he wasn't standing on nothing. Nothing at all. His feet was six inches off the ground. Them buckskin britches had shrunk so fast they'd lifted him clean off the ground by them straps under his feet.

"'Brother Joe,' I says to him, 'you better come down from there.'

"'Brother Bill,' says he, 'I'm scrooching down as hard as I can.'

"'Brother Joe,' says I, 'try scrunching down.'

"'Brother Bill,' says he, 'I'm scrunching, too!'

"But it wasn't no use, for in a minute he was floating so high I couldn't reach his feet."

"Merciful gracious!" Widow Harris gasped. "Merciful gracious on my poor old head!"

Bill continued. "I says to him, I says, 'Brother Joe!'

" 'I'm still here, Brother Bill,' he says, 'but I'm going up.'

" 'Try swimming through the air over to that little tree,' I says to him, 'and catch ahold of it.'

"So that's what he did. Joe just paddled like crazy through the air, and pretty soon he got hisself over to the sapling.

" 'Hang on tight,' I says.

" 'I'm hanging,' Joe says. He sure enough had grabbed hold of that sapling, 'cause I heard a creak and a screek, and I saw that tree come right up by the roots. Then it popped right out of the ground, and Joe sailed up higher.

" 'Brother Joe,' I shouted. 'Catch this knife and cut loose your britches.' And I threw up my barlow knife. He caught it, and he began to saw away at the first strap, the one under his right foot. Then there was real trouble. When that strap gave way, Joe's right leg shot down out of his britches leg and the other leg shot up because there wasn't nothing holding against it. He just started whirling, slow like, at first. Since the one strap was pulling him sideways, he came spinning down on the ground. Just turning like a pinwheel."

"But whar's Joe now?" the Widow Harris persisted.

"That's what I don't rightly know, Mrs. Harris, ma'am," sighed Bill. "The last I seen Joe he was whirling across the fields like a wheel with the rim off, right out into the west."

Pat
and the Sarpint

Kaintuck, a hunter from Kentucky, looked across the campfire at Pat. "Do you mean to sit there and tell me that you never seen a snake?" he asked.

"Divil a one," answered Pat, who was a big, strapping Irishman with a face as red as his hair. "Don't yez know that blessed Saint Patrick drove them all out of Oireland into the sea before I was born, so he did?"

"Well," asked the third man around the campfire, "don't you even know what snakes look like?" His name was Tarheel, because in those days almost anyone who came from North Carolina was called a "Tarheel."

"Sure and they look like wurrums, isn't it now?" said Pat.

"Worms!" roared Kaintuck. "If you see a worm as thick as your arm and as long as your leg, with teeth as sharp as carving knives, you'll have seen a pretty fair example of a snake!"

"Mother Machree," whispered Pat in terror.

Now if you think it is strange that there could be an Irishman or anyone else in America who had never seen a snake, you must remember that this story took place a hundred years ago. That was the time when potatoes stopped growing in Ireland, and Irishmen came to America by the hundreds of thousands. The Irishmen knew as little about America as Americans knew about Ireland.

As soon as Tarheel and Kaintuck saw that Pat knew nothing about snakes, they thought they might have a little fun with him.

"Of course," said Kaintuck, after sitting and thinking awhile, "there are little snakes, too. You take this hook-and-eye snake, now. This little feller breaks himself up into tiny pieces that look like bits of sticks. They wiggle over to you, then they hook themselves together again and give you the most infernal bite."

"Go on with yez," grinned Pat. But he did squirm a bit, and he brushed away all the twigs he could reach with his coat.

"Aw, Kaintuck," protested Tarheel. "You ought not to scare Pat with talk about hook-and-eye snakes. There's none of them around here. Leastwise, I ain't seen any. I seen some rubber snakes, though."

"What in the howly name of Oireland are thim?" asked Pat.

"Aw," said Tarheel, "they're just stretchable snakes. They've got skin like rubber bands, so they don't have to crawl up on you. They just fling themselves out and give

you a dig with their fangs. If you ain't full growed, they
jerk you right off your feet when they snap back."

"Begorra!" shuddered Pat. "I hope we don't see the
least bit of thim!"

"I saw a corkscrew snake this morning," said
Kaintuck, "but I didn't want to say anything for fear of
scarin' you, Pat."

"For the love of heaven, what are corkscrew snakes?"
Pat asked, his hands shaking.

"Aw, they're just little bitty snakes. They won't hurt
you at all, unless they get on you," replied Kaintuck. "I
knew a feller down in Virginny who got a corkscrew
snake in his hair. Before he could pick it out, it bored
through his head. It didn't come out till three weeks later,
and then it came out through his foot. Nearly tickled him
to death, it did."

"Bad luck to the two of yez," growled Pat. " 'Tis
humbuggin' me, yez are."

But Kaintuck and Tarheel put on the most honest-
looking faces you ever saw, and told Pat that every word
was the truth.

"Naw," mused Tarheel, "you ain't got no cause to be
scared of corkscrew snakes, neither. They can't crawl
straight, being like corkscrews. But them hoop snakes,

now, they's bad uns. You can't run away from them. They grab their tail in their jawbones and roll after you like a hoop. They's bad uns, they is."

"Arragh, now, what sign of a fool do you see on me?" Pat compained. "Do yez think it's daft I am to believe that squit? Come on, now, gintlemen, give over!"

"Give over what?" Tarheel protested, with a pained expression. "Just because you ain't got no snakes in Ireland, you think we ain't got none here? We got snakes I ain't even thought of yet."

"All right, Pat," said Kaintuck, "we won't tell you any more stories about snakes, but you ought to know about the bell-tailed rattlesneak. That's one snake you have to look out for, the bell-tailed rattlesneak. They're all around here in these woods."

"You mean rattle*snake*, don't you, Kaintuck?" objected Tarheel.

"No, I mean rattle*sneaks*. They're eight feet long and they got bells on their tails instead of rattles. Only trouble is they're sneaky. They don't ring their bells till they pitch into you."

"That's the plain, uncooked truth, Pat," Tarheel agreed. "They're fierce. They've got long green tushes that drip pizen. Green pizen. I saw one of them whip at a man and miss him and bite a tree instead. That thar tree just swelled up and bust like lightning hit it."

"Mother Machree!" said Pat. "Sure and I don't want to hear any more about snakes, sure and I don't. It's goin' to bed, I am."

Pat got up, muttering about the liars a man meets in

the mountains of Tennessee. He made up his bedroll, and Kaintuck and Tarheel noticed that he was mighty careful about scraping and sweeping a clear place to put it. Then Kaintuck began singing "Springfield Mountain," an old song about a man who was bitten by a "pizen sarpint."

"Arragh, give over, will yez?" grumbled Pat, wrapping himself in his blanket. He was a good-natured man, and he didn't mind the teasing. But he feared for the grain of truth in it.

Kaintuck and Tarheel sat by the fire until Pat began snoring. Then Kaintuck said, "I've got an idea how to make Pat remember bell-tailed rattlesneaks the rest of his life. You take this little saddle bell and hold it while I fix him up a snake."

Kaintuck went over to his pack and took out a length of rope. He greased it well with deer lard until it was all slithery and slothery. Tarheel grinned when he saw what Kaintuck had in mind.

Kaintuck took the rope over to where Pat was sleeping. He quietly and carefully lifted the blanket off Pat and tied one end of the rope to his shirttail. Then he rolled the rest of it up in a coil and put it under Pat's shirt, right against his skin. He turned and whispered to Tarheel, "Now, when I jab him with my fork, you start ringing that saddle bell. Are you ready?"

Tarheel nodded and whispered, "I'm ready."

Kaintuck took his fork and jabbed it hard into Pat's ribs three or four times, yelling "SNAKE!" with each jab.

Pat rose straight into the air about ten feet. "Huh-wee! HUH-WEE! Howly Oireland! Machreeee!" When he hit the ground his feet were whirling like two pinwheels. He spun around the camp like a tomcat with his tail on fire.

"Oh, murther! Murther! Japers!" Pat roared. "Sayze him! SAYZE HIM! Sayze him by the tail. Oh, howly harps! Take him off before he swallers me alive. TAKE HIM OFF! I'm pizened from head to foot by the reptile! Whisht, whisht, whisht! Tear him into jabletts! A wha! Och, murther! He's forty foot long!"

Pat buzzed around the campfire like a bumblebee stuck in a bucket of tar. The rope flew out behind him like the tail of a kite. On one trip around the fire, the loose end of the rope fell into the flames and took light.

"Och, japers! JAPERS! He's a FIERY sarpint! Ho, murther! He's got a light now to see how to bite me! Och, help, will yez? I'm swallered, I am, entirely all but me head! He's sixty foot long!"

All the while Tarheel rang the bell furiously and Kaintuck yelled "Snake! Snake! SNAKE!" But the two pranksters were so doubled up with laughing that it was all they could do to say anything. Tarheel laughed so hard he fell on his back and waved the bell around like a baby with a fit. Kaintuck hugged a tree with both arms and a leg, trying to stand up, and shouted "SNAKE!" whenever he could catch a breath.

"Snake! SNAKE!" screamed Pat, taking up Kaintuck's cry. "Oh, gintlemen, save me, will yez? Will yez try to save me? He's eighty foot long if he's an inch. Shoot him, can't yez? Shoot him! But don't aim at his head, for he's got half me body in his mouth! Shoot! SHOOT! Ninety foot! Save me, will yez?"

Pat ran around and around the fire and then finally straight into the woods, forgetting all about the hoop snakes, corkscrew snakes, and hook-and-eye snakes among the leaves. Kaintuck and Tarheel writhed and rolled on the ground, unable to stop laughing.

"Snake! Snake!" Kaintuck gasped, weakly. And Tarheel gave the saddle bell a tinkle whenever he could take his hands off his aching sides.

The last sounds they heard out of Pat were "Yeeech! Murther! Och, Mother Machree! Snake! A hundred foot long! SNAKE! Shoot 'im! Shoot 'im! Snake! Snake!" And then these cries finally died out in the distance, as Pat and the rope ran out of Tennessee.

A Tough Bird

In South Dakota one night some cowboys were sitting around a campfire eating a hot, savory stew. Cookie, the camp cook, had just served it to them from the chuckwagon. The men were tired and very grateful for the chance to rest and fill their empty bellies.

Then under that star-ridden sky came a great, whooping "Gee whillikers!" from Eatumup Jake. He held his face in his hands and moaned. "That there was the *toughest* piece of meat I ever did have 'tween my jawbones. Cookie! Cookie!" he shouted. "Come over here before I rattle your brains with your own saucepan."

Cookie just reached into the chuckwagon and took out a big iron skillet. Then he walked over to Jake. "What's your trouble, Jake?" he asked, with an idle twirl of the skillet.

Eatumup Jake didn't answer until he had felt his teeth with his fingers to make sure they were all in place.

"Gee *whill*ikers!" he said again. "What on earth was that meat in the stew? I've been eating cowboy food for twenty years and I *never* had anything so tough in all my borned days!"

"Prairie hen," replied Cookie.

"What is prairie hen?" Eatumup Jake asked.

"Prairie hen is a kind of bird they've got here in South Dakota."

"Has it got wings?"

"Yep. Sort of wings."

"Serves me right," said Jake, sadly. "Should have knowed better than to eat anything with wings that abides in this country. But why couldn't you have cooked it different?"

"I cooked it the way it's supposed to be cooked," replied Cookie, drumming his knuckles on the skillet. "I plucked the feathers off it and nailed it to a board. The whole thing was boiled till the board was soft, and then I threw the prairie hen away and served up the board in the stew. Must have left a piece of prairie hen in the pot and that's what you was probably chewing on. But none of the others fellers complained. Did you, fellers?" He turned to the rest of the cowboys sitting around the campfire, looking at them with a very sour look. Then he swung that big iron skillet back and forth. "Well?" he asked.

"Nope," they all said.

"Well, I got more bones'n usual," complained Dilberry Ike.

"Them wasn't bones," growled Cookie. "Them was just

ordinary splinters from the board. You get 'em in every stew. Nothing to complain about."

"It's exercise that makes them prairie hens so tough," said Billy Bull. "Exercise is what makes tough. If you see a tough little boy, you know he's had lots of exercise. It's the same with a prairie hen. They're runnin' around so hard, scratchin' up enough to eat, that they just get tough."

"Billy Bull," Dilberry Ike said, "that's the real truth. Exercise is what makes tough. It reminds me of being a young un down in Colorado. My daddy had a fighting rooster so fierce and tough and feisty that he out-fought every rooster in the county. When there weren't no more roosters to hack at, my daddy's rooster used to come up from the henhouse and wallop the barn with his spurs. One day, my daddy came in with his boots and chaps all tore up. That there rooster had lit into him like a mad cat. So Daddy said he was going to put that rooster to some good use for a change. He said we was going to eat him.

"Daddy got himself an ax-handle and went down to the henhouse. My daddy was a big feller, and when he hit that rooster with an ax-handle, well, that rooster stayed hit.

"My mama took that rooster and put us kids to work plucking the feathers off him. It took us all day, even using the crowbar on his tail feathers. Mama boiled him all night, but next morning that rooster was as tough as he was the night before. So she put him back into the stew-kettle and boiled him till the end of the week.

"Seems like the more she boiled that rooster, the tougher he got. Daddy tried to cut him up with the butcher knife, but the knife couldn't cut him. Mama tried to stick him with the fork, but the fork couldn't stick him. So Daddy just grabbed hold of that tough bird and started chewing. He gnawed and chawed a while, then he gave out a screek.

" 'Daddy, did you bite him?' we asked. 'Did you get a bite?'

" 'I got the jaws-ache, that's what I got,' my daddy howled. So he picked up that rooster by the feet and carried him down to the woodshed and slapped him down on the saw-bench. Then Daddy set up the big buzz saw and run that rooster right into it. BRANNNGGG! went the buzz saw, and sawteeth just flew all over the woodshed!

"Daddy said a few words that I don't rightly remember

no more. Any other man in the county would have given up, but Daddy didn't quit so easy. He'd shot a possum the night before, so he decided to cook the rooster once more and add the possum. My daddy thought the one would soften up the other. Six hours the possum and the rooster boiled. Then Mama took them out and made a meat pie out of them, and *baked* it.

"Oh, glory!" Ike went on, after a deep sigh. "How I recall that pie. I remember how good it smelled. And I remember when the pie came out of the oven, Daddy said, 'Dern your hide, old rooster, I bet I softened you up *this* time!'

"Just then the pie crowed TUCK-TUCK-TUCKA-ROOO! and everybody jumped. Daddy gave me a wallop across the ear, thinkin' I done the crowing. When I was a boy, I could give a first-class imitation of a rooster crowing.

" 'It wasn't me, Daddy,' I bawled out, but Daddy, he gave me another good whop. 'Mind your manners!' he said. And with that he took up his dinner knife and stuck it into the pie. When he did that, there was just the darndest, most *etarnal* spittin' and sputterin' in that pie, and every bit of that possum came flying out in little pieces. And then . . . . ."

Dilberry Ike stopped and reached for the coffeepot. He poured himself a cup of coffee without saying another word.

"Well?" asked Eatumup Jake. "What happened then?"

"Why, that rooster just stuck his head through the crust, crowed, and strutted out to the barnyard," said Ike. "That's what happened."

Water on the Brain

What? You never heard of *Scott*? *Martin* Scott? *Captain* Martin Scott? Why, you might as well not have heard of Ethan Allen or Molly Stark.

Martin Scott was born in Bennington, in the green state of Vermont, where turkeys gobble through the butternut trees and the air is always fresh and crisp. He loved the forests and the long valleys that were full of game to hunt with his great Vermont rifle.

If you could talk with the animals of Vermont, they would tell you about Martin Scott. They would tell you that he could throw two potatoes into the air and shoot one bullet through the two of them. They would tell you how he once put a ramrod into his rifle, instead of a bullet, and shot six pheasants at the same time, and the hot ramrod roasted the birds like they were on a spit in a barbecue. They all knew Martin Scott better than they wanted to. Yes, indeed they did. Whenever they heard his boots clumping through the leaves, they took to their heels and their paws and their hoofs and their wings, every time.

Martin Scott was as happy as a butterfly in summer, except for one thing. A bear. Not any old bear, but a special bear named Old Growler. He was as big as a bull and as tall as a chimney. His claws were long and curved and sharp, like the sickles Vermont farmers use to cut bushes. He was as savage as a meat-ax from his teeth to his toenails, and he was smarter than any other bear in the forest. When Captain Martin Scott was out hunting game, Old Growler would wait until he knew the Captain had used up all his bullets. Then he would lumber out of the bushes and steal whatever Captain Scott had shot, before the Captain could turn around. And Old Growler would laugh a big bear laugh, "Owf! Owf! Owf!" and walk away with everything.

Captain Scott always howled with rage when Old Growler did that. But he was never able to do anything about it.

One day in the autumn of the year, when the leaves of the maple trees had turned the green hills to a fiery red, Mrs. Scott asked her husband to go out and shoot a turkey for their dinner.

One turkey was not enough for Captain Scott's dinner, for he liked to eat as much as he liked to hunt. So, when he saw a turkey perched high on a limb in a dead tree and a deer on the hill behind it, he didn't know what to do. Mrs. Scott wanted a turkey, and he liked to please his wife. But he wanted the deer, and he liked to please himself sometimes. Of course he couldn't shoot one without frightening the other away.

"Now, there's a puzzle," Captain Scott thought. A great hunter must think fast, and it was not more than the time it took the turkey to blink its eyes before Captain Scott knew what to do. He put two bullets into his rifle, one on top of the other. Then he raised the gun and shot the turkey with the first bullet. Before the second bullet had time to leave the barrel, he pulled down the rifle and shot the deer! And what do you know? The first bullet went right through the turkey and split the tree open, and there was a beehive full of honey for the Scotts' dinner!

"Well," said Captain Scott, "that's almost a good meal."

He piled the deer and the turkey and the honey on his back. But the load was so heavy that when he lifted it his suspender buttons popped off like bullets, and one killed a rabbit that had been foolishly watching from the bushes.

Captain Scott laughed. "What a fine appetizer that will make!" And he put down the deer and the turkey and the honey to get the rabbit. But when he came back with the rabbit, there was nothing left but the tracks of a monstrous great grizzling bear. Old Growler had sneaked out of the woods and had taken all the game, including the honey, which bears love more than anything else.

"I'm going to get that grizzling bear before sugaring time," vowed Captain Scott, "if it's the last thing I do."

And when he got home empty-handed, Mrs. Scott allowed as how Old Growler was sure making a fool out of the great Martin Scott.

Later on that winter, when the snow had come to stay and the cold wind blew icicles from the top of the Green Mountains through the hemlock trees, Captain Scott met Old Growler once more. It had been a fine day of hunting for the Captain, and he was coming home with his game bag full and his bullet bag empty. But for Old Growler it had been a bad day. He had found nothing to eat, and he was as angry as a bear. He was too mean to sleep through the winter, like other bears, and this made him worse than ever.

When he heard Captain Scott's boots sloshing through the snow, Old Growler pounded the earth with his great paws, breaking branches and shattering stones. He burst out of the woods and jumped in front of Captain Scott.

"Gr-r-r-r!" roared Old Growler.

"Gr-r-r?" answered Captain Scott politely. Suddenly he remembered that he had no bullets. He was so frustrated that he began to cry.

Martin Scott cried so hard that tears poured from his eyes in big round drops. They rolled down his cheeks and onto his beard and froze into balls of ice.

"Why, they're round and hard like bullets!" he exclaimed. As soon as he had said the word "bullets," he had a clever Vermont idea.

"Gr-r-r-r!" The ferocious old bear roared again. He rushed at Captain Scott, swinging his sharp claws like a scythe. But Captain Martin Scott raised his rifle, slid a frozen teardrop bullet into it, and BANG! He shot that great grizzling bear plumb smack between his big, brown, ferocious eyeballs. Down fell the bear, dead as a doornail.

"How surprised Mrs. Scott will be!" smiled the Captain to himself. "She never thought I could get Old Growler. Now she will just have to say that I am truly the greatest hunter in all of Vermont."

But what do you suppose? When he had pulled Old Growler home, Mrs. Scott would not believe him.

"No, sir, Captain Scott," she laughed. "A big, grown man like you shouldn't tell fibs. If you had shot that bear, there would be a bullet in him. And there isn't. There's nothing but water. Old Growler died of water on the brain!"

Slow Train Through Arkansas

All the locomotives are gone now, and it is a pity. How wonderful it was to be a child when trains were tugged along by those huffing and puffing and chuffing and whistling locomotives! In daytime you could see the plume of smoke racing along the horizon. At night if you looked out of your bedroom window when the lonesome whistle drifted through the darkness, you could see the red firebox burning against the black sky.

More than anything else, it was those steam trains that built this great country. The long steel rails and short crossties, like giant zippers, fastened the nation together. They stitched the coasts to the mountains and the mountains to the plains and made one nation out of the bits and pieces of states.

Of course there were some trains that didn't stitch the country together so much as they tied the country up. Like that slow train through Arkansas half a hundred years ago.

Why, there was one fellow who really thought the *Arkansas Cannonball* was going someplace when he bought himself a ticket. All Mr. Charlie Brannan wanted to do was to travel to Morrow.

"You have a town called Morrow on the line, do you not?" Mr. Brannan asked the ticket agent.

"Oh, yes," said the ticket agent briskly. "You want to go to Morrow?"

"I want to go today and come back tomorrow."

"You can't go to Morrow today and then come back tomorrow. You should have gone to Morrow yesterday and come back today, because today's train to Morrow is gone for today."

"Well," Mr. Brannan persisted, "I have to go to Morrow today so I can get back tomorrow."

"Now look here," said the agent impatiently. "How can you go anywhere tomorrow and get back again today?"

"All right," sighed Mr. Brannan, "give me a ticket to Morrow, and I'll travel halfway there today."

"Well, that will put you on the next train, mister," said the ticket agent, and he sold Mr. Brannan a ticket.

Mr. Brannan climbed aboard the *Arkansas Cannonball* an hour later.

"Neighbor," he said as he sat next to a man, "let me introduce myself. My name is Charlie Brannan, and I'm from Charleston. I'm a stranger here, and I'd like you to tell me something about this train."

"Good to meet you, Mr. Brannan. Thomas Quinn is my name. I've been riding this train ever since I was a little boy. I got on at Selma and I hope to get to Siloam Springs at the other end of the line before I die."

"Is that what the initials of this railroad mean, 'Siloam Springs and Selma'?"

Thomas Quinn nodded with a grin. "They tell us that *SS & S* means *Siloam Springs and Selma*, but all of us old-timers say it means *Slow, Stagger, and Stop.*"

"Well," said Charlie Brannan, "I've noticed that this is no ordinary train. For instance, there isn't any cowcatcher at the front of the locomotive, but there is one at the back of the train. Why is that?"

"Neighbor, this train never hit a cow in all its history. Cows walk too fast for it even to catch up with them. But the cows kept climbing aboard the last car and strolling up the aisles, butting the passengers. So, the cowcatcher was just taken off the front and put on the back."

"That sounds logical," remarked Charlie Brannan.

"Yes," agreed Thomas Quinn. "But it has its drawbacks. We had a real drawback on this line once with that rear-end cowcatcher when a cow got her tail caught in it. She was frightened, somewhat, and she just ran down the track, pulling the train backward. As far as anybody could remember, that was the fastest the *Arkansas Cannonball* ever went."

Before Charlie Brannan could comment on that story, there was a sudden commotion up ahead in the coach, and Mr. Brannan and Mr. Quinn stopped their conversation. The conductor was arguing with a Dutchman.

"I von't pay dot much!" declared the Dutchman.

"Then you'll have to get off the train," the conductor replied firmly.

"Den I get off," said the Dutchman. "I valk!" He left his seat, walked up the aisle, and stepped off the train. All the passengers looked out their windows to watch him. He got on the track ahead of the train and began walking briskly. The train was moving so slowly that in a minute he was a couple of hundred yards ahead of it. The engineer blew his whistle.

"You can vissel all you vant," the Dutchman shouted, turning around, "but I ain't coming back!"

"Will the train have to go this slowly all the way because he won't get off the track?" asked Charlie Brannan.

"Slowly!" said Thomas Quinn. "The engineer has the train going full speed now, just to scare him!"

The conductor just moved on down the aisle and stopped at a seat where a woman and a young man were sitting.

"Tickets, please," he said to the woman. She handed him two tickets.

"One of these tickets is only half fare," the conductor complained. "Half fare is for children."

"Yes, that half-fare ticket is for my son here," the woman replied.

"But he is a full-grown man!" protested the conductor.

"That may very well be," insisted the woman, "but he was a boy when he got on."

The conductor shrugged and continued down the aisle. Then he noticed something out the window, so he stopped and put his head out. He waved to an old man limping along the side of the track with a crutch, and called out to him.

"Mr. Lincecum!" he shouted. "Come aboard and I'll give you a free ride home."

"No, thank'ee," the old man called back, waving his crutch. "It's only a couple of miles now, and I'm in a kind of hurry." In a moment he had limped out of sight ahead of the train.

By and by a station appeared along the road ahead. Charlie Brannan turned to his companion and said, "Mr. Quinn, I have the most certain feeling that this train is going too slowly for my purposes. I think I'll just get off and find some faster means of transportation. Why, this train is just a place to stay!"

"I'll get off, too, and keep you company, if you like," said Mr. Quinn. "I could use a short walk around town."

"Oh, no, I couldn't let you do that," protested Mr. Brannan. "You'll be left behind."

"No concern there," said Mr. Quinn. "The *Arkansas Cannonball* won't be farther than the bend in the road by the time I want to ride again."

The two men stood up and put on their coats. As they took their suitcases down from the rack the conductor came by.

"Congratulations, conductor," Mr. Quinn said, with a chuckle. "Take this cigar as a token of my admiration and gratitude."

"What's that for?" asked the conductor, looking puzzled.

"Well, sir, I have been riding this train for nearly twenty years, and this is the first day it has been on time. I think you deserve some little reward."

"I'd appreciate having the cigar," the conductor said, "but it wouldn't be right for me to take it. You see, this is yesterday's train."

Davy Crockett's Worst Experience

The year was 1827, and the city was Washington, in the District of Columbia. The city, and the nation, were still very young. The people had fought against the frontier and its dangers. Now they were settling down to run the country in a quiet, ordinary, civilized way. That is, a few people were settling down. They could be found in Washington, D.C., and a few other cities along the east coast of the young nation.

Beyond the Great Smoky Mountains life was still a mite wolfish. And the people were still a bit wild. One of them, a backwoodsman from Tennessee, was elected to Congress in 1826. The Easterners were anxious to know all about this rip-tailed, roaring fellow. They had heard he wore a coonskin cap and carried a ferocious, long rifle that he called Betsy. So they sent a young reporter to interview Colonel Davy Crockett.

They met where people from Congress gathered, at a lemonade bar in the city of Washington. "Just what was the worst experience you ever had, Colonel Crockett?"

Davy stood Betsy up against the wall and rubbed his bristly chin. "The worst experience I ever had?" he repeated. "Wal, now, that's a mighty hard question. Mighty hard. I fought a lot of hoss-alligators, human and otherwise, and nary a one but didn't bite a chunk of my nose or a piece of an ear or gouge out an eye or two. They was all tough, they was. But I'm a rip-tailed roarer, born in the backwoods . . . ."

"Born in the backwoods," repeated the newsman, as he wrote down what Davy was telling him.

"Born in the backwoods of Tennessee," continued Davy, with a glowering look at the reporter for

interrupting him. "And I was raised by a grizzly bear. I got nine rows of jaw-teeth and holes punched for more. I got a double coat of hair, steel ribs, wire intestines, and a barbed-wire tail, and I don't give a dern where I drag it. I can walk like an ox, run like a fox, swim like an eel, fight like a bear, and spout like a whale. So none of them hoss-alligators never bothered me to no great extent."

"But Colonel," interrupted the young reporter, "what was . . . ?"

"Hold your tongue, you tarnacious varmint, or I'll jump down your gullet and gallop your insides out!"

"Yessir, Colonel Crockett, sir," the young reporter said, looking a mite quivery. Colonel Crockett was the first backwoodsman he had met, and he was taken by surprise.

"Wal, now, whar was I before you so totaciously interrupted me?" Davy asked. "Yas. I was grinding my brains, trying to think what was the worst experience I ever experienced in all my experience.

"Course, you can't believe everything you hear about me. Some of it don't make good sense. Some of it don't even make good *non*sense. Like that tale about me swallerin' a bolt of lightning. It's a brass-bound *lie*, mister! I never had no truck with lestrissity. It was a quart of coal oil I swallered. It like to burnt my innards out and my outtards in. Felt like it was seven bull buffalo kicking around inside me. So I made a long wick out of my socks and swallered that and proceeded to burn that oil off. Whoop! And I burned like an oil lantern! Fer ten minutes I was the brightest man in three counties!"

Davy stopped to swallow a ripstaving gulp of lemonade, as if he were thinking about that hot coal oil, so the reporter got another word in edgeways. "Colonel Crockett," he asked, "some people say that Terrible Tom Dowdle, the ferocious hoss-alligator, was your equal in rough-and-tumble fighting. Is that true?"

"*Tom Dowdle*!" exploded Davy, blowing his lemonade over half the room. "*Tom Dowdle*! The ragman? A child, sir, a child. Old harmless Tom Dowdle! Now, sir, you take me. I am the gen-u-wine article, and I can out-run, out-

swim, and out-drink-more-lemonade than any man in this
or any other locality. I can scream through my nose! Tom
Dowdle? I unjointed his neck with one jerk. I ground his
bones into buckwheat flour!" Davy paused, took another
sip of lemonade, and added softly, "As a matter of *fact*,
mister, I never met him."

"We heard you fought bears single-handed with bare
knuckles," prompted the reporter.

"I did, indeed I did, I did," agreed Davy. "And I did it
with both hands tied 'round behind me. I used to do it

regular-like, on cold mornings, just to wake up proper. I recollect I was out in the woods one cold morning and I didn't have my bowie knife or Old Betsy with me, nothing. And the biggest, ugliest, *grizzling* bear you ever seen jumped me. I just grabbed him 'round of his middle and hugged him a *leetle* bit and then I stuck my thumbs in his eyes and bit off a piece of his nose, just as I would do with *any* man. That bear lit out like a hound dog with a mouthful of porcupine. Bears ain't much for biting and gouging."

"Well, Colonel Crockett, that sounds like a terrible experience. But not your worst, I take it. Is that right?"

"No, sir, I reckon maybe pre-haps my worst experience was with them painters."

"Painters?" gasped the reporter. "You mean to say the great Davy Crockett had trouble with painters? Men who paint houses? or pictures?"

"Fellow citizen," said Davy gently to the reporter, "I'm talking about varmint painters. Wousers! Catamounts! Mountain lions! Cats as big as hosses, with butcher knives for claws and railroad spikes for teeth! Painters!"

"Oh, yes, Colonel," said the reporter, smiling. "Now I understand. You mean panthers."

"Yes, that's what I said, painters. That was a bad time, it was. I reckon it was the worst, indeed I do. Why I was just plain exfluncticated! Wouldn't have been so bad if I hadn't been sick with yeller janders. Or if I hadn't been so long far into the woods that all them painters could gather like ants at a picnic. Thar was only about a dozen of them painters to start with, so I loaded up Old Betsy and took aim at three or four of 'em. But that was the onliest time Betsy let me down. She sputtered and spootered and sizzled and fizzled, but she wouldn't go off. So I took out my bowie knife and I fought 'em for a while, but yeller janders makes a man's skin tender, and them butcher-knife claws scratched me up something fierce!"

"Gracious!" exclaimed the reporter, shuddering.

"Yas. Fierce! And then all the painters in half the nation heard the squealing and the squalling and come to join in. Must have been nigh on to eight hundred and seventy-four of them altogether. I couldn't count 'em exactly because it was getting dark. But I know I saw seventeen hundred and forty-eight fiery red eyes blazing in the dark. Oh, hoss, they was *fierce*! They wasn't *human*!"

"Good heavens!" shivered the reporter. "What did you do?"

"Do? *Do*? What could a person do? There wasn't a tree around for miles, far as I could see. But I climbed one anyhow. It was only big around as your neck, and when them painters started scratching and clawing it, the tree shook and swayed like a daisy flower. And I couldn't get high enough to do me much good, seeing that it just had one branch, and that was only six feet off the ground. Them painters kept jumping up and swiping and wiping me with them butcher-knife claws till my leather britches was scratched clean *off*. I tell you, hoss, it was a good thing it was night time, because it was downright *un*-decent. And the more they jumped and scratched, the madder they got."

"Colonel," asked the reporter, "why didn't you just grin them away, like the time you grinned at the raccoon and missed, and grinned the bark right off the tree?"

"You've heard of that, have you? Wal, I tried grinning them painters away but it was so dern-fire dark they couldn't see me. A big black grizzling bear come up to see what all the fuss and the flapdoodle was about, and they et him alive. Chawed his bones to flinderjigs. Oh, they was a mean-mad passel of kitty-cats."

"Succotash!" whispered the reporter in awe. "That was a *bad* experience!"

"Oh, it was worse'n that. Them thar painters was so mad they couldn't get more'n a couple-three feet peeled off my hide. Why, they jumped up and down in particular *fits*. And I'm telling you, young hoss, Colonel Davy Crockett started to commence to begin to become just a *leetle* bit concerned about his situation. For reasons of health, you understand.

"I knowed if them painters cotched hold of me, they would devour me faster than an alligator could swaller a puppy dog. Wal, with all that scratchin' and chawin' and gnawin' and bitin', that tree trunk just started to *give*. It bent a little bit and then it bent some more, and pretty soon it was bent over like a buggy-whip. And there was Colonel Davy Crockett — that's me — hanging down from it. There wasn't nothing old Davy could do, it looked. And then that trunk snapped. It snapped half in two. And down I went, right into that passel of painters."

"Gee-hosophat!" the reporter exclaimed. "How did you get away? What did you do?"

Davy stopped for a moment and shook his head as he recalled this worst of all experiences. He filled his glass with lemonade and drank it right down.

"I didn't do nothing, that's what."

"Well," persisted the reporter, "how did you escape?"

Davy wiped his lips on the sleeves of his buckskin jacket and looked hard at the reporter. "I didn't escape," he said. "They ate me. They ate me *in*-tire."

John Henry

Down in the coal-mining country of the Appalachian Mountains, you can see the biggest machines in the world. One of them is called a surface-mining shovel. It is so large that it would be hard for you to see all of it at once.

It is higher than a twenty-five-story building. It has an enormous mouth called a dipper. This dipper is set with great steel teeth, each as big as an automobile, and it bites off great pieces of rock and chews them up so that men can get at the coal.

Some people say that machines like this are too big, and that they push man out of his natural place on earth. And they are afraid that machines are becoming too clever. But these people who fear machines do not know about John Henry. As long as there are John Henrys in the world, we do not have to be afraid of machines.

The night John Henry was born the sky turned as red

as a copper kettle. Lightning reached down from the sky like branches of a silver tree. The clouds rumbled and the earth shook. And John Henry's father shivered and said, "Glory! There's a great man just born somewhere, for that's the way the sky carries on when a great man is born!"

He didn't know it then, but his son was going to be that great man.

John Henry's mama nursed him and fed him cornbread and buttermilk and turnip greens. Soon he was a mighty big baby. Then one day, as he sat on his mama's knee, he looked up at her and said, "Hammer be the death of me, Mama, hammer be the death of me."

His mama was so startled she nearly dropped him. But she knew then that her John Henry was a special baby.

She watched him grow each day until he was soon bigger than his daddy.

"Daddy," said John Henry one day, "you got to teach me to be a steel-driving man. That's my life work, Daddy. I know I got to die with that hammer in my hand. Nothing I can do about it."

John Henry's father didn't know what to make of that, but he said nothing, because he knew by then that John Henry was no ordinary boy. So he got John Henry a long-handled, sheep-nosed sledgehammer and told him about driving steel.

"Little Johnny boy," he said, "you take this hammer. Then you get a shaker man to hold a hard steel drill down on the rock. Then you swing your hammer up 'round your shoulder and WHOP! You drive that steel on down into the rock. Then the shaker — he shakes 'cause he's scared you going to hit him with that hammer — he turns the steel 'round a little bit, and WHOP! You hit it again, and soon you drill a hole in that rock. Then you be a steel-driving man."

"But Daddy," asked John Henry, "what they want to make holes in rocks for?"

"Little son, the dynamite men put dynamite in the holes and they blow that rock all to smashereens. Then they can get at the coal."

That was all John Henry needed to know about steel driving. By the time he was grown to be a man, he was the biggest, strongest, fastest steel-driving man in the whole state of Tennessee. It was hard work, swinging a nine-pound hammer from sun-come-up to sun-go-down.

But John Henry liked hard work. It made him feel good to have his muscles grow. He would come home at night and eat a big dinner of chitterlings, ham hocks, blackeye peas, and flitterjacks, and then go to bed. His body grew a little bit bigger each night, and next morning he was ready to drive steel harder and faster than he had the day before. As soon as the rooster crowed, you could hear a *Wheeengg!* and that was John Henry's hammer ringing against the steel and echoing across the mountains.

Each time he swung his hammer back over his shoulder he would give it a twirl, and the sheep-nosed hammerhead spun like a button on a string. Then he would swing it down like a whip. Oh! It was something joyous to watch!

But as time went on, some clever men invented machines to do a man's work. One man took four wheels and a small steam engine and put a hammer on the front of it, and that was the first steam drill. He tried it out against some ordinary human steel drivers, and the steam drill always beat them. Its hammerhead would bob up and down like a woodpecker, *whump-a-whup, whump-a-whup, whump-a-whup,* as it chewed through rock. The captains of the work gangs got to fearing this steam drill. The machine was too good, they said. There was no place for the steel-driving man any longer.

Then one day John Henry's captain told him, "I'm going to bring a steam drill around here, John. And I'm going to show you how to whop steel."

"Humph!" laughed John Henry. "I'm a natural man. No steam drill can beat a natural man." And to show the captain what he meant, he swung his hammer around his shoulder and WHOP! Men in Memphis hundreds of miles away heard the rumble of the shiver of the ground, when John Henry thumped that steel.

But the man who invented the steam drill, he didn't quiver at the quake. "A man ain't nothing but a man," he said, when he brought his steam drill to John Henry's job. "Before you beat this steam drill of mine, John Henry, the rocks in the mountain will turn to gold!"

John Henry curled his lip and his eyes flashed lightning like the skies on the night he was born. "Captain," he said, "you can bet your last penny on me, because I'll beat that steam drill to the bottom by sun-go-down."

The steam drill just nodded its iron head and went softly *"whump-a-whup, whump-a-whup, chump-come-up, dump-the-pup."*

"You talking to me, steam drill?" asked John Henry softly, and the lightning was in his eye.

"*Munch-you-up, munch-you-up, munch-you-up.*"

"You won't munch *me* up, steam drill," whispered John Henry quietly. "You the first of all machines to fight against a natural man. I'll fight you for all us steel-driving men. If you win, we all work for you. If I win, you steam-drill machine will work for us. What you say, machine?"

"*Good-enough, good-enough, good-enough,*" the steam drill chuffed.

The man who owned the steam drill poured in some water and shoveled in some coal. John Henry stripped off his shirt, and his muscles glistened in the sunshine. He reached down and took some earth in his hands and rubbed it on his hammer handle. He took a deep breath and shouted, "Captain, get some men coming with new-sharp steel! And everybody get out the way. When I swing this hammer 'round my shoulder, you bound to hear her ring!"

The captain shouted loudly, so everyone could hear. "John Henry and the steam drill are going to race. They're going to drill one long hole each when I give the signal. They'll keep going until sun-go-down. Then we'll see which one has drilled the deepest hole. Are both of you ready?"

"WHUMP-A-WHUP!" pounded the steam drill.

"Let's go!" roared John Henry, and then he raised his hammer up toward the sun.

"Go!" shouted the captain.

The mountains moaned and the ground groaned with the pounding of the steam drill and the whopping of John Henry's hammer. The stone dust flew out of the holes in the rock so thickly that you couldn't see John Henry or the steam drill. All you could see were the men running in and out of the clouds of dust. Some carried water and coal to the steam drill, and some carried sharpened drills to John Henry. Every few minutes a new shaker would come in to spell the man who held John Henry's drill.

The dust from the drills rose up to the sky like thunderheads and turned red as blood against the hot sun. The earth shivered and the men's feet tingled from the pounding of the hammers on the earth. And all the time you could hear the WHUMP-A-WHUP of the steam drill and the WHOP! WHOP! WHOP! of John Henry's hammer.

At last the sun slipped down the western sky and rested just atop the hills. The captain called out, "Quitting time! Quitting time! Pick up your tools! Workday's done!"

The dust settled and the captain took out a long, thin measuring rod.

"I'm going to measure the holes now. Everybody look close, so we don't make a mistake."

He put the measuring rod down the hole drilled by the steam drill. "Nine feet!" he called out. "The steam drill made nine feet!"

The workmen who had been watching shook their heads sadly. "Poor John Henry," they said. "No natural man ever made a hole that deep with a hammer in one day!"

The captain went over to the hole John Henry drilled.

He slipped the measuring rod down to the bottom of the hole.

"Fourteen feet! FOURTEEN FEET! My lordy-lord! John Henry beat the steam drill!"

The men all jumped about and shouted and cheered, for a natural man had beaten the machine. No machine would scare them again. The men jumped about and cheered wildly for John Henry, but nobody saw John Henry hang down his head and slip to the ground. His great chest shook and his great heart broke, and he died, there, with his hammer in his hand. Right at that moment the sun flashed strong as it dipped into the mountains and turned all the rocks into gold.

What Are Snipe?

The Mississippi is a wide river, and long too. It was a popular route for comfortable steamboats, around the time Dory and I rode the *Mary Douglas*. We were travelling down river just to see what New Orleans had to offer two gentlemen from Illinois.

One afternoon, Dory and I met in the lavender lounge for tea and for the river sights. Just as Dory got to talking about hunting snipe, a strange man sat down at our table. He was dressed in a vest, belt, boots and hatband all made of alligator hide. We could tell that he was interested in our conversation. But he did not say a word, not even to introduce himself. He just listened to Dory talk about snipe hunting.

Well, all of a sudden this alligator man spoke up.

"Sir," says he, "what are snipe?"

"Snipe are the best game that fly," Dory answered him. "They're about as long as your foot, and they have long thin legs and bills like an ice pick. They're dusky-colored, more than anything else. You usually find them in marshes or swamps, hiding in the grass in the daytime. But at sundown they rise up, flying this way and that way, and their wings hum like . . . ."

"Stranger," said the alligator man, "you can stop right there. I've seen the critters. I know 'em like an old boot."

"Well, then," continued Dory, "you know what good eating they are."

"Tar my feathers!" exclaimed the alligator man. "Do you Yankees really *eat* them things? I always heard that you Northerns did some funny things, but eating them pesky snipe is more'n I ever heard of."

"Of course we eat them," answered Dory. "What would be the use of shooting them if we didn't eat them?"

"Drot my skin! We kill 'em right enough down in Louisiana, but we just swat 'em."

Dory looked as if he thought swatting snipe was about as foolish as you could get. But he acted polite enough and just said, "I suppose you are right. The snipe go south to Louisiana for the winter so there aren't enough of them to shoot."

"Stranger," said the alligator man, "we have 'em summer, and winter, and all the seasons in between. And there's so many of 'em that a man can hardly pole a pirogue through the swamp. Two of my boys were on the riverbank chopping wood the other day, and those snipe were singing so loud the boys thought a camp meeting was goin' on up river."

"Snipe singing?" asked Dory, looking puzzled.

"Well," said the alligator man, "I'm an alligator hunter, sir, and there's times I'm in the swamp hunting gators when I hear a singing goin' on, like the kind a bull alligator makes. Well, when I turn around it's nothing but them pesky things you call snipe that's making all the racket. Stranger, if you'll only come down to my plantation and shoot off the crop of snipe I have there, I'll give you the best load of alligator hides you'll ever see."

"Well," said Dory, "what could be more ideal? Hunting snipe is worthwhile in itself, but getting snipe and alligator hides at the same time is more than I can resist. Where do you live?"

"Just downriver a bit. It won't be no trouble at all for you to get there. And if you'll only kill off them pesky snipe, you'll be my everlasting, eternal friend forever! Those infernal things pitched into my young un the other day, and his head swelled up, big as a pumpkin!"

"Pitched into your child?" asked Dory, excited to hear that snipe were so ferocious in Louisiana. "I never heard of them attacking anything but insects before. Pitched into your child, you say?"

"Dod drot my skin if they didn't. And my child was lucky to get away with nothing more than a swollen head. Why, four of them things'll carry off a dog."

Dory shook his head in wonder. "Snipe carry off a dog?" he asked. "Snipe?"

"Yes, snipe," said the alligator man. "What you Yankees call snipe, anyhow. Down in Louisiana we call 'em mosquitoes."

Cats

"I should think it would be lonely for you way out here," said the city man to the old prospector. "This is the only cabin I've seen in three days of hiking."

"Yep," agreed the prospector. "Ain't many people in this part of Californy. Leastways, they ain't livin'. There's lots of dead uns just over these here Panamint Mountains, down in Death Valley. But they don't make much company fer an old-timer like me. No sir, I get all my company from my pets, Lord love 'em."

"What kind of pets do you have?" the city fellow asked, warming his hands in front of the wood stove. It was cold inside the cabin, for there was a row of holes right along the outside walls. Each hole was as big as a bucket and the cold air poured in, like water through a sieve.

"I got all sorts and shapes of critters fer pets," said the prospector. "Depends a lot on what time of year it is. Now it's turnin' cold agin, I'll be roundin' up my winter snake."

"A winter snake? What kind of snake is that?"

"Oh, just an ordinary snake. Rattler, or sidewinder, or something. I don't know. He's just my winter snake. Soon's it freezes outside, that snake turns stiff as a stick and I use him to poke up the fire. Warms the snake up, too. He likes that."

The city fellow shivered a little. The very mention of snakes always gave him the shivers, and it was getting colder by the minute in the cabin. He looked again at the line of holes in the walls. They looked like a row of little doorways, but he couldn't imagine what use they had.

"What are all those holes in the walls?" he asked finally. "I should think it would be a lot warmer in here if you closed them off."

"Can't close 'em off. I need 'em fer my cats. I got cats the way some people got mice. Twenty-four cats, so there's twenty-four holes for 'em to come in and go out."

"But wouldn't one hole do? Couldn't the cats go out one by one?"

"Mister," replied the prospector, taking his pipe out of his mouth and looking sternly at the visitor, "when I say *Scat,* I mean SCAT!"

"But what do you keep so many cats for?" persisted the city fellow.

"I need 'em fer my cat pianner."

"What on earth is a cat piano?" the city fellow asked.

"A cat pianner is a pianner made with cats. It's a musical instrument. A man has to have some music once in a while. Good for your education and culture too."

The city fellow looked at the prospector doubtfully.

"Yes, I know what a piano is, but what is a *cat* piano?"

"Well," sighed the prospector patiently. "You get a box about one foot wide and one foot deep and six foot long. Then you drill a row of one-inch holes in the top. Then you get a mess of cats, half of 'em black and half of 'em white. You pop 'em in the box and stick their tails out through them holes. The white tails are the natural notes, like the white keys on an ordinary pianner. The black tails are the sharps and flats. Ain't you ever seen a pianner?"

"Yes, but not with cats in it."

"Well, what's the matter with cats in a pianner? You got somethin' agin cats?" The old man glowered at the city fellow.

"Of course not," the city fellow hurried to assure the prospector. "I just have no idea how a person could play a cat piano."

"You can pull the tails with your hands. That's one way. Or you can put the cat pianner on the floor and stomp on the tails, the way you play a player pianner. Just stomp on whatever note you want. Learn it in no time. Pretty soon you get to trompin' and stompin' and dog my cats if you can't make beautiful music. Course, you got to arrange the cats right. You got to put the big ones where the low notes is and the little ones where the high notes is."

The city fellow snorted. "Oh, come on, old fellow! You're just having fun with me! You show me this cat piano and I'll believe it."

"I can't show it to you."

"Why not?"

"Had to get rid of it. The dog kept jumpin' in and outten the box. He got the cats so stirred up I couldn't keep the blamed thing in tune. Made the most infernal racket you ever heard." With that, the prospector got up and put a stick of firewood in the stove. He turned to the city fellow and said, "Think mebbe I can take up my mouth organ agin, now the dog's gone. I sure admired makin' a little music with the mouth organ. But I give that up, too."

"Why?"

"Dog didn't like it."

The city fellow rubbed his hands together over the stove. He didn't know what to make of all this talk of cat pianos and poker snakes, but he had to say something, so he asked, "That must have been a good dog for you to keep him, considering all the trouble he caused. Was he a hunting dog?"

"Tarnation if he wasn't a huntin' dog!" said the prospector. "He was a good hound. Just about the fastest dog I ever saw. Last time we had a thunderstorm he chased a streak of lightnin' and bit it three times 'fore it could get out the yard. He was so good a huntin' dog I didn't need a gun. I just sent him out by hisself. If he heard me talk 'bout possum, why, he'd bring back a possum. If I talked 'bout a raccoon, why he'd bring me back a raccoon. Yep, I miss that dog, good old feller."

"What happened to him?"

"Nothing, I don't guess. I reckon he's out there on the track somewheres. I made the mistake of lettin' him hear me say I was so hungry I could eat a horse. I reckon he's out there trying to drag a horse home."

"Hmmm," the city fellow reflected. "So that leaves you with just the cats now, does it?"

"Yep. Got only them pianner cats and an old-timer cat, Old Wood Leg."

The city fellow stared at the grizzled old prospector. "Old Wood Leg? Do you mean the cat has a wooden leg?"

"Yep. Old Wood Leg has a wood leg. Got his real leg bit off by an elephant."

"But there aren't any elephants in California," protested the city fellow.

"I never said there was any elephants in Californy," the prospector retorted, looking angry and impatient. "Old Wood Leg and me, we used to hunt elephants in Idyho. That's where he got his leg bit off."

"But there aren't any elephants in Idaho, either," insisted the city fellow.

"I know there ain't any elephants in Idyho, stranger. I know there ain't. You don't have to tell me somethin' I know. There ain't no elephants in Idyho because Old Wood Leg and me, we killed 'em all."

"Well, old man," the city fellow said with a great sigh, "if you tell me there were cat-eating elephants in Idaho, I hate to think what you'll tell me next."

"Why, I'm goin' to tell you the truth, same as I just done. I'm goin' to tell you that Old Wood Leg is the *only* wood-legged cat in the entire Panamint Mountains. I made the leg myself. I took 'bout four inches offen the end of a broomstick, I did, and strapped it on the cat. Worked fine, too, once he got used to the new way of killin' rats. He had to catch the rat and hold it down with his good paw while he beat the varmint silly with his wood leg."

The old man sat down and looked gloomy. "I hate to say this about a good friend like Old Wood Leg, but I'm gettin' mighty impatient with him. I guess it's old age settin' in on me, but I can't stand all that stompin' around the house. That wood leg makes the most *infernal* racket. A man can put up with just so much. There's a limit to everything."

"Yes," said the city fellow, getting up and putting on his coat, "there is a limit to everything. I think I'll be on my way."

"Stranger," said the prospector as the visitor stepped through the doorway, "keep your eye open fer my dog, will you? If you see him, tell him to forget about that horse."

"Are you sure he'll understand me?"

"Oh, he'll understand you, right enough. I'm just afraid he won't believe you."

The Courtship of Sam Snaffles

Nearly everybody in Clinch County, Georgia, thought Sam Snaffles to be a pretty tolerable sort of young man. Merry Ann Hopson thought a good deal more of him than that. To her, he was the dearest, kindest young man in all the world.

But there was one person in Clinch County who had a very different view of Sam Snaffles. That person was old Squire Hopson, Merry Ann's father. And that was bad, because to Sam Snaffles, Merry Ann Hopson was the dearest, kindest young lady in all the world and all he wanted was to make her his wife.

One soft summer evening, when it seemed that all the world was pleased with itself and everyone else, Sam Snaffles asked Squire Hopson for his consent to marry Merry Ann.

"No!" roared the squire. "No, indeed, sir!" The squire shook his head violently. "You are not the proper sort of young man for my daughter. Oh, I've been observing you for a long time. I saw where you were lacking. And it isn't only my opinion. I asked your horse, and he told me the same."

"My horse?" asked Sam, looking puzzled.

"Yes, sir, your horse. I asked him about you. And he said, 'Look at me, Squire Hopson. I don't have an ounce. of spare flesh on my bones. You can play my ribs like a piano. Sam doesn't have but five bushels of corn in his corncrib, and he's such a monstrous big eater himself that he'll eat four of them and think it's mighty hard to give me the other one. Sam's got no money, Squire, that's his trouble. No money.'

"Yes, sir, Sam Snaffles, that's what your horse said. And you can't set aside my opinion and his both. It's a fact you don't have any money, and no man without it marries my Merry Ann. So good evening to you, and don't come back until you get some money!"

Poor Sam. He didn't say another word, for he knew the Squire was right. What made him sadder was knowing his horse looked down on him for having no money.

"There isn't anything for me to do now," Sam said to himself, "but to ride off and get some money, or lose myself to Merry Ann forever." He got up on his horse and gave the animal a dozen sharp kicks in the ribs for telling the old Squire he didn't have any money. He stopped by his cabin, picked up his rifle, and set out for the great swamp.

Sam hunted all day, but it seemed all his luck had

turned against him. Just after sunset he came to a lake
so large he could barely see across it. There he decided to
rest for the night. He lay under a tree and fell asleep.

When he woke it was night, the darkest night he had
ever seen. Not a star was shining, yet the sky seemed to
be full of shapes even blacker than the night. And he
heard a great roaring noise, as if the world were coming
to an end. He rubbed the night sight into his eyes and
looked hard into the sky. Geese! Hundreds of thousands
of them! More than any living, breathing, human being
had ever seen in all the history of the earth — and there
they were, circling around, settling on the lake.

"Well," thought Sam, "if a man could only get all those
geese into one net, wouldn't he have some money!"

As soon as he let that thought run through his mind,
Sam set his head to figuring how he might catch a few
thousand of those birds. He knew that the geese would
stay at the lake for a few days before they set off for the
southern part of the world. So he leapt into the saddle

and galloped to the town of Haylow. There he hired a mule and wagon and all the ropes and floaters and fish-hooks and other tangly things a man would need to net a thousand geese.

When he returned the next day, the geese were off on some business of their own, so he stretched his net right across the lake. Every part of the net had a plowline tied to it, and every plowline lay in Sam's hand. "When those geese light on the lake," he thought, "I'll just whip those plowlines around a tree and pull them in. If I could just catch five hundred of them, I'd sure enough have some money."

While he was counting his imaginary geese and imaginary money, the geese began drifting back through the sky. Like little gray clouds, they came down in small formations and settled on the lake. They played and splashed and screamed, and dived in the water. Then Sam carefully pulled in his net. "Fifty thousand of them I have — not five hundred!" he chortled aloud. But Sam made a mistake, for the geese heard him and beat their wings to take to the sky again.

The net was around them and when all fifty thousand geese rose up, they took the net with them. Sam wrapped the lines around what he thought was a tree by his side. But when he began to rise off the ground, he realized he had wrapped the ropes around his leg. In a moment he was flying through the air. "The money's got me!" he cried out.

Mile after mile the strange kite, with Sam as a tail, sailed across the sky. After a while Sam felt that he was slowing down. The geese were beginning to tire. They beat their wings slower and slower. They dropped lower and lower. And soon Sam could feel the top branches of trees brush past his legs. A few minutes more, and the fifty thousand geese and the net and the ropes and Sam Snaffles were all down in the forest, tangled in the trees. The geese screamed their rage, but Sam laughed, for just about twice out of sight, he could see the lights of the city of Waycross, flickering through the trees.

"Hurrah!" he sang out. "Merry Ann, we'll have money after all. I can sell the fifty thousand geese right here!"

Some few days later, Sam Snaffles rode up to Squire Hopson's house on a new horse, one that wouldn't tell tales about him behind his back. He had on a new suit, and a new shirt with a stiff collar four inches high, and a bright-blue tie. Looking at him, a person might think he had money.

But Squire Hopson was not to be fooled by appearances. When Sam knocked on the door, the old Squire frowned at him. "So it's you again, is it, Mr. Snaffles?" he asked. "Do you think new clothes and a new horse will make me believe that a good-for-nothing like you has money? Who lent them to you?"

"Squire Hopson," Sam said sternly, "never mind about that now. I have business to talk over with you first."

"Business!" snorted the Squire. "What kind of business could you have with me?"

"Squire Hopson, you owe a certain amount of money, say a thousand dollars, to Dr. Columbus Mills. Is that right?"

"That's business between Dr. Mills and me, sir. You have no business in my business, and I'll thank you to mind your own business."

But Sam went on. "You gave this house as security, didn't you, Squire, if you couldn't pay the loan?"

Squire Hopson looked very black with anger. "That, sir, is no business of yours. Dr. Mills did lend me a thousand dollars some years ago, and I put this house up to him for security. But that business is between him and me."

"Oh no, sir," replied Sam. "The business is between you and me. You see, Dr. Mills has sold the debt to me. And unless you can pay me the thousand dollars, why, I am afraid you will just have to move out." With that, Sam showed him the bill of sale, all signed by Dr. Mills.

"You see, Squire Hopson, you are living in my house now."

"Great fishhooks!" shouted Squire Hopson. "Do you mean to turn me out of my house headlong?"

"Well, sir," replied Sam, "I can't have my house occupied by a man who has no money. If you had money, you could have paid Dr. Mills that thousand dollars. Moreover, Squire Hopson, I had a little talk with your horse, and he told me the same thing. 'Sam,' he said, 'Squire Hopson is an old fraud. He lives in that fine house and acts as if he owns the world. But a man can't hide much from his horse. And I can tell you, Sam Snaffles, that old Squire Hopson doesn't even own the rocky chair he sits in.'"

Squire Hopson began to tremble with fear, for he knew his horse had told Sam the truth.

Sam went on. "So, sir, as soon as I heard that, I took a little bit of my money and I went to Dr. Mills, and I bought your debt. So now I own this house."

"What about your love for Merry Ann?" asked the Squire, his lips quivering. "Are you going to throw her and her poor old daddy out?"

"I love Merry Ann with all my heart, Squire. I aim to marry her, and she aims to marry me."

"What's to become of me?" wailed the Squire.

"Well, now," said Sam, "I reckon any father of Merry Ann's is a father of mine, even if he hasn't any money. But there's one thing I won't tolerate again, Squire."

"What's that, Sam Snaffles, sir?"

"Don't ever go talking to my horse again," said Sam.

Conversation on a Rooftop

It was floodtime in Missouri, and the river was fifty miles wide. Two men sat on the roof of a farmhouse, listening to the water lapping around the eaves.

One of the men appeared to be the owner of the house. He was a farmer dressed in his work clothes — blue overalls, a faded blue shirt, and a floppy canvas hat — and he was chewing on a wet straw, the way farmers do when they are thinking about something. He didn't seem to mind the floodwater licking at his feet. You could tell he was used to such things.

The other man was dressed in clothes that were very neat and natty, for he was a traveling salesman, or what they called a "drummer" in those days. He traveled from town to town, selling everything and anything to storekeepers. He was thinner and smaller than the farmer, and he seemed to be much more upset by the flood than the Missourian was.

"Where did you say you come from, mister?" asked the farmer.

"I come from the Oklahoma drylands. That's where a man doesn't have to sit on his roof to keep his feet dry."

"Don't you ever have floods in Oklahoma?" asked the farmer.

"Floods of dust, that's all. Oh, sometimes the dust gets to be the least bit damp, but not often," the drummer sighed. "As a matter of fact, it's so dry where I come from that we catch fish by tracking their dust clouds."

"It's different here," said the farmer. "The game warden don't let us go fishin' when the river's up. The fish get so confused they can't find the river, and it just don't seem fair to pick 'em off a windowsill when the water's high."

At this point the farmer stopped talking to smile and wave at two women who were floating past on some furniture. "Good day, Mrs. Wilson," he called out. "Hello Sally. Nice day."

"Friends of yours?" asked the drummer.

"Acquaintances, more like. Mrs. Wilson — she's the older one sitting on the table — she sings in the church choir. The other one — accompanying her on the piano — is her daughter Sally."

The two men sat silently for a while after the women had drifted away down the flooded river. The farmer went on chewing his wet straw. The Oklahoma drummer rubbed water off his shoe with his handkerchief. He was very wet and uncomfortable, and still amazed at so much water.

"Yep," said the farmer, "there goes my chicken coop again. Every time the river's up that coop just up and floats around the farm."

"But the chickens are still in it!" said the drummer.

"That's just fine," said the farmer. "All that rocking makes 'em lay better."

"I suppose that when the water goes down this land around here is pretty rich," the drummer observed.

"Richest land in the U.S. and A.," agreed the farmer. "Why, the Missouri soil is so rich that corn comes up the day after it's planted. There's a rumbling all night long, like an earthquake, and a little green shoot the next morning."

"It's different in Oklahoma," said the drummer. "Our land is so poor that if a pig finds a blade of grass, he has

to call two other pigs over to help him pull it out of the ground. It takes all three of them to cast a shadow, they're so thin. Yes, it's mighty puny country we have over there. And our dogs are so weak they have to lean up against a fence to bark."

"Here in Missouri," the farmer continued, "the only thing that makes us weak is water on the knee."

"We wouldn't mind a little water on the knee out in the Oklahoma drylands," said the drummer. "We could drain it out into the riverbed."

"Riverbed?" asked the farmer, cocking his head. "Do you have a river? Thought you said it was dry."

"Oh, yes, we have a river," the drummer smiled, "but we only get water in it every couple of years, if it happens to rain. And even then it's so shallow that if you water your horse the river drops three or four inches. Our rowboats are made so light that they'll float on a heavy dew."

A chicken floated by, its head and tail seesawing as it balanced on a board. The drummer looked at it, and his jaw dropped open. "Did I see that chicken right?" he gasped. "It looked to me as if it had webbed feet!"

"Yep," said the farmer. "It had webbed feet. All the chickens 'round here have webbed feet. How do you s'pose they get around the barnyard?"

"Well, now," said the drummer, shaking his head, "that's a caution. That *is* a caution. Over where I come from the ducks see so little water that we take them in the house if it rains. They'd drown if we didn't." He rubbed some more water off his shoes. "Yessir, no rain

makes for mighty poor country. That Oklahoma drylands is so poor that wheat hardly makes it out of the ground. The sparrows have to kneel down to get at it. And then they have to be very careful the wind doesn't blow them clear away."

"You have big winds out there, do you?" asked the farmer.

"Big winds! Why, just an ordinary breeze blows the cows so flat against the barn that we have to peel them off like wallpaper. And when a farmer plants seeds he has to hold his foot on them till they can take root. Why those winds can blow a farm clear out of the state and back again the same day."

The drummer peered over the other side of the roof. "What on earth is that?" he asked, looking bewildered.

The farmer looked around. "Where?" he asked.

"Over there." The drummer pointed to where a hat was moving along in a straight line, then turning right around and moving back.

"Oh, that. That's my neighbor Jackson. He swore he'd plow his field today, come drought or high water. Wet goin' for his horses, though."

The farmer threw his straw in the water and stood up. "Well," he said, "the flood won't go down much more this afternoon, so I reckon I'll go do my chores. The old woman will be wantin' the catfish out of the mousetraps and a fire lit so's she can make supper. Proud to have you eat with us, mister."

"Thank you, but no," said the drummer, as he got up and brushed off his trousers. "I'd better be on my way. I'll just stroll downtown and see if I can sell your town an irrigation system."

And he stepped off the roof.

1 2 3 4 5 6 7—U—82 81 80 79 78